CLEANING GOLD MINE

The entrepreneur's blueprint for hidden Golden Nuggets

Joe Darden

Zofaa Publishing
Atlanta, Georgia

© 2018 by Joe L. Darden II

ISBN-13: 978-1986535137

ISBN-10: 1986535134

Published by
Zofaa Publishing
www.zofaapublishing.com

All rights reserved. Written permission must be secured by the publisher or author to use or reproduce any part of this book, either in print or electronically, except for brief quotations in the book reviews or news articles.

Contents

Chapter One – Value Creation Opportunity?   5

Chapter Two – The Power of Vision   12

Chapter Three – The Cleaning Industry is a Goldmine   22

Chapter Four – Decision Makers   31

Chapter Five –   The Power of being Consistent   40

Chapter Six – How to Start a Business   47

Chapter Seven - The Joy of Entrepreneurship   73

Chapter Eight – Entrepreneurial blueprint for Success   79

Chapter Nine -The Art of Selling   83

Chapter Ten - Why Work With Our Cleaning Company   90

Work With Us -   95

Chapter One

Value Creation Opportunity?

Anytime there is a business opportunity the first question you should ask is how do I define the value creation opportunity?

In other words, how much money can I make? It depends on how hard you work and how much effort you put into growing your business.

You could earn $20,000 to $100,000 or even $1m. It really depends on you. Your time means something to you. You don't want to spin your wheels chasing something that at the end of the day is a low value creation opportunity.

You want it to be worth your while. So, the question becomes what form of market analysis do I need to engage in to better understand the value creation opportunity. Once I understand that I pull together the right level of energy to go pursue that or not. So that's the first decision you have to make.

Why Should You Start A Janitorial Cleaning Business?

Why the janitorial business? Because it's an incredibly simple business that makes a lot of money, will always be in demand, and requires very little investment. And if you do it correctly, you can be making money very quickly.

Consider all of the positive advantages of the janitorial business -- As you read these, compare and understand how very different these advantages are from those of most other types of businesses:

√ I can't state this loudly enough – the janitorial business is high-profit, repeating income. When you do a good job for your customers, you get new checks from them month after month, year after year. I have one account I've been with since 1983, and that one building has literally paid for our homes, our vacations, and put our kids through private schools.

√ Because janitorial has such low operating costs, you can build your business at your own pace, and scale it to any size -- whatever is comfortable for you. You can keep it small and make an extra thousand or two a month or put the pedal to the metal and make it as big as you want. You don't have to have a lot of accounts to make a healthy income.

√ You can run your business from your home, giving you the lowest possible operating costs and all kinds of home-office and self-employment tax advantages. And you don't need storage space - your equipment and supplies can be locked up in your customer's buildings.

√ Every building needs cleaning. Your customer base is unlimited.

√ The janitorial industry is highly recession-proof. My business has always grown, even during the worst recessions. During every recession, at least a few of my customers ask me about my business, and they usually start by saying something like, "So, the cleaning business just keeps on rolling, doesn't it?" (lol, yes it does).

Maybe you're old enough to remember the 2000-2001 recession? The January 2002 issue of Cleaning & Maintenance Management Magazine has an article called "What Recession?", and while the article is a few years old, it does show how recession-resistant the janitorial business really is. The article is based on a poll called the "Contract Cleaner's Statistical Survey".

√ Despite the recession, 57.6% of the respondents said their sales increased an average of 20.7% over the previous year.

√ Incomes of owners of commercial janitorial services rose 15.3%, to an average of $85,600 per year. (note - adjusted for inflation this would be $107,000 in 2015).

√ The statistics showed that commercial office cleaning services are the most profitable type of cleaning business - far more profitable than house-cleaning.

√ The respondents were overwhelmingly independent business owners (only 4% reported being a franchise).

√ You can "duplicate" yourself and multiply your efforts by hiring employees to do the work for you. You can have a "more-than-full-time" business, yet work part-time hours.

√ You don't need to buy any of the things that most businesses require -- no lease on an office, no storefront, no display cases, no inventory.

√ You can run your business in the evenings and weekends, after your regular working hours - it doesn't require that you quit your day job. You can do what I did when I started my business – after building my business for a year I told my boss that I couldn't afford to keep working for him.

√ You have multiple sources of income because you have multiple customers.

√ Once you've signed up a new customer, you don't have to "sell" to him again because you keep servicing his account over and over. Compare this to a real estate agent who may never sell another house to the same person again, or an attorney who may never do legal work for the same person again. They need fresh new names and faces every day.

√ Cleaning office buildings is much easier than house cleaning, because there are no kids or pets to clean up after, and there are very few "cleaning surprises" in office buildings. If you want to go crazy, try cleaning people's homes (I tried it for one month, and vowed to never do it again). And building managers and owners are much easier to deal with than home-owners.

√ If the idea of dealing with professional business-people scares you, don't worry - the vast majority of professional business-people are some of the easiest people to deal with you'll ever meet -- especially building managers. It's one of the qualities that makes them professional.

√ Janitorial is a $120 billion-dollar industry in the U.S., and continues to grow every year.

√ The growth projection for janitorial between 2015 and 2025 is higher than the average of all other industries.

This is an industry with a very bright future -- and now you can get in on it in a way that will allow you to start making money almost immediately.

And finally, why should you build your business using my System? Because while everyone else just gives you advice, I give you a toolbox full of pre-built systems -- and no one can get you making serious money faster, cheaper, or easier.

You're doing great! Keep reading!

"Definitely doing well with the business, I am making about $3000 a month. My business is 5 months old, and I have been invited to bid on a building in Dallas in about 2 weeks that looks to be worth about $2000 a month. Before I found you, I had spent about $200 for books from other people who said they could show how to start this type of business, but they were nothing compared to yours. I had previously bought the book written by the man who said you don't need to bring a vacuum, I laughed at it when I read it and I really laugh at it now. And I can see that just the money I will save on my taxes this year will pay for your program about 3 times over. I believe 100% that this is the best money I have ever spent" Paul L., Irving, TX* (JanQuest Note: $36,000 a year in 5 months, with the possibility for $60,000 a year coming soon).

What is the value creation opportunity?
_____
_____
_____

Is it worth my time?
_____
_____
_____

Chapter Two

The Power of Vision

Imagine a person walking aimlessly. That is the life of a person without vision.

Vision is one of the key factors in the entrepreneurial blueprint. It is impossible to win in life or business without a clear vision.

When I started my cleaning business a few years ago, I started with a clear vision in mind. I had a sense of where I wanted to see my business in the next few years.

A clear vision is an immeasurable advantage to any person. Without the eyes we fumble about in darkness. Great leaders have vision burning inside them. Nobody else can hold that flame for them.

Don't give up on your entrepreneurial dream. Hold on tight. Your vision will not lie. It will come to pass. Life will try you; circumstances will harass you, and troubles may come as a thief in the night. Yet, stay on! Have you ever dreamed of something fabulous but it never happened? You were so convinced of it materializing, giving it all you have. You were disappointed, disgusted and disenchanted. Hey, my friend, don't give up on your vision! It's all you have! See it again!

Albert Einstein failed many times and had plenty of reasons to give up, but he didn't. He had learned to dream again despite the failures.

Vision in motion

Vision is the ability to see from within to create success and make a positive impact.

When you look within, what do you see? How do you hope that your life turns out? What would you like to change about your life or your world around you? The answers to these questions are great clues about your Life Vision. When God enables a vision God mobilizes the provision to bring the vision into fruition.

We have to see it first before we'll receive it.

See it where? In our imagination, soul, mind, spirit (heart) or whatever you like to call it. I will use imagination or spirit for the context of this book.

One of my all-time my favorite TV shows was 'Rebel Billionaire' with Sir Richard Branson. That was the first time I met Sara Blakely, an unusual lady with a vision. Here's her story:

Sara Blakely started out selling copiers and fax machines door-to-door and was frequently escorted out of office buildings for cold-selling. Like so many people, Sara dreamed of an entirely different career and life, but she was waiting for her bright idea.

One night Sara cut the feet out of her pantyhose to wear with white pants and open-toed shoes and, at that moment, Sara knew she had a million-dollar idea. Seven years later, this former salesgirl turned her $5,000 investment into more than $150 million in retail sales, 55 employees, 100 different styles of Spanx, four patents, and ASSETS, a new brand at Target. Sara is turning her attention to giving back by helping women globally.

Sara joins the judges' panel on American Inventor as a true inventor alongside George Foreman, Peter Jones, and Pat Croce on a mission to find, "The Next American Inventor". She recently gave a one-million-dollar check to Oprah Winfrey for her all-girls leadership academy in South Africa.

That is how a clear vision can transform a life forever.

Three types of people

1. Those that are vision driven
2. Those that lack vision
3. Those that don't know how to accomplish the vision

Vision is more than physical sight

Vision far exceeds physical sight. It is the light of life. The story of Helen Keller exemplifies this fact. Helen Keller was blind and deaf at nineteen months of age. She had several struggles in her life while growing up, but her vision of becoming somebody significant surpassed her lack of physical sight. In 1904, at the age of 24, Keller graduated from Radcliffe *magna cum laude*, becoming the first deaf and blind person to graduate from a college. Keller went on to become a world famous speaker and author.

She is remembered as an advocate for people with disabilities, as well as numerous causes. In 1915, she founded Helen Keller International, a non-profit organization for preventing blindness. Keller and Anne Sullivan traveled all over the world to over 39 countries, and made several trips to Japan, becoming a favorite of the Japanese people. Helen Keller met every US President from Grover Cleveland to Lyndon

B. Johnson and was friends with many famous figures including Alexander Graham Bell, Charlie Chaplin and Mark Twain.

Big vision leads to a big life

The size of your vision determines the size of your life. Small vision will yield a small life; a big vision will produce a big life.

Vision brings life to a lifeless situation, sees a fetus in the womb of the medically proclaimed barren, holds a lemon but sees lemonade. It is the hope of the hopeless.

The good news is that there is a huge vision God has for your life. Your life was meant to be meaningful. God has plans and purpose that he wants to accomplish through you.

The greatest asset you can ever have is to discover God's vision for your life.

How to discover your Life Vision
A step by step Approach

Find a serene and quiet place. Carry nothing with you except a notepad (or journal) with a good pen. Eliminate distractions such as bright light, noise or other people activities. Sit comfortably. Say a prayer to God to help and guide you. The prayer could be as simple as "Dear heavenly Father, thank you for the gift of life. Help me to know your vision for my life. Amen."

Close your eyes and imagine the life you want. Write down what you see- the thoughts, ideas, pictures, events or occurrences that come to your mind.

Circle any three that fit with your passion and desires. Strike out the others. Those three have become your Life Vision. That's what you want to achieve with your life.

More applications in discovering your life vision

1. What you love so much, you would do for free.

2. The Mother Theresa Principle: Whose pain do you feel?

3. Write down the three biggest goals of your life.

4. What frustrates you so much you'd like to change it?

5. Have you tried praying & fasting?

6. Observe your strongest gifts and strengths.

7. The problem you love to solve.

8. What profession, vocation or career excites you most?

9. Frankly, what do you want to do with your life?

What vision will do in you

1. Your Life Vision is your purpose.
2. It will bring order in your life.
3. Vision will bring focus into your life.
4. Vision will generate discipline in your life.
5. Vision will develop character in you.
6. Vision will promote patience in you.

What vision will do for you?

1. Vision will bring you personal fulfillment.
2. Vision will cause you to choose your friends.
3. Vision will inspire you to leave this world a better place.
4. Vision will push courage out of you.
5. Vision will tell you that you're unstoppable.

Beware of vision killers

Vision Killers will always come to test your faith in your dream. Is there anyone in your life that pleasures in talking you down? Whenever you talk to or are with this person, you begin to feel little, uncomfortable, incompetent or average? Stay away from anyone or anything that that attacks your vision. Remember that your vision is your life.

The sacrifice for vision

It will cost you something to become somebody. Sadly, there are a lot of people are around running with a deceptive message of sit-and-do-nothing and become rich, attract wealth into your life by using the "Law of Attraction", work smart not hard. I will be honest with you. Success does not happen without some form of sacrifice and hard work. Your vision will require you to sacrifice something. Athletes work long hours training and preparing for games. Michael Jordan in his peak days, regularly rose in the morning and shot free throws for two to three hours every morning.

Most successful people have to let go of something to achieve their Life Vision. Bill Gates gets up at 4:00am. Get a compelling vision for your life and business and you will be on your way to great success.

2. Get a Vision

See It

What are you living for?

What are you trying to create?

What will it look like? (Think specific: colors, brand, personality, and purpose)

What do I want to achieve?

...In 1 year?

___

…In 5 years?

___

___

___

…In 10 years?

___

___

___

What do I need to achieve these goals?

___

___

___

Chapter Three

The Cleaning Industry is a Gold Mine

My story is one of setbacks, tragedies, being told that I couldn't be successful, overcoming obstacles, being constantly overlooked, having to struggle and hustle for opportunity. I had to take time to identify who I was and what my purpose was.

On the journey of facing insurmountable setbacks, I became bullet proof, tough, focused, committed and determined. "Without struggle there is no progress." - Fredrick Douglass. I became immune to being told No, being told I wasn't good enough or I wasn't worthy enough. I kept focusing on advancing not only through life, but to correct the incorrect things that I needed to become successful.

Before entrepreneurship even became an idea, I had an identity problem of knowing who I was, and what I was called to do on the earth. So, for years I would struggle with just getting ahead being able to put a clear path together of what I wanted to do in life and why I wanted to do it. As I stated in chapter one, if you don't have a vision in life your life will become a constant rat race. When you deal with thoughts of inadequacy, developing a vision can become mission impossible.

The open doors of self-mastery

I made a commitment to have Self- Mastery at the center of my being. Improving every area of my life became the fuel needed to remain hungry and humble.

My children and wife have been a game changer for me, they have made me want to level up my life, my imagination, my drive, and my dreams. Raising the bar on myself hasn't been easy but it was necessary to experience growth personally and professionally.

When my first child was born in 2004, I went back to school to obtain my Master's degree in Business. I remember like it was yesterday, I still had no earthly idea of what I wanted to do, but I knew that I needed to make money to provide for a growing family.

One night in class, a fellow student struck up a conversation and told me that by starting a Commercial Cleaning Franchise I could make a lot of money. So, I looked at the opportunity and got started. It required me working long hours after I got off from my job. Tired and weak, I forced myself to learn the business.

Although I was struggling initially to develop a vision or create an opportunity for myself, opportunity found me all because I made the decision to work towards self-mastery. Whenever you make a decision to do better and become a better you, you allow creative power to work on your behalf.

Let the mining begin

It took years to learn the process of cleaning or more specifically, how to clean buildings effectively. Aside from learning how to clean effectively, there were many skill sets that were required to make the business a success. These skill sets are not exclusive to the cleaning industry; they are skill sets that will cause any business to flourish. One of those skill sets is developing solid relationships. Solid relationships are especially important in the cleaning industry. Part of the reason why this is necessary is because you must sell yourself before you can sell your company.

As an employee you are not required to learn many different skill sets other than the ones that pertain to your job. So, if you're on a job for 10 or 15 years your skillset will be concentrated and inadequate if you decide to make a change to your career.

I was able to learn the skill sets required and needed to operate a successful business, things like marketing, sales, being able to handle Nos, rejections, prospecting, customer service, relationship building skills etc. When we as people have good paying jobs I think it makes us weak to some degree. It causes us to be devoid of striving to grow in different areas of our lives and skills. Lucky for me I had a sneak preview of what personal development could do for your mind.

I was constantly reading books, listening to audio and podcasts while driving, turning my company vehicle into a University on wheels.

Great communication skills show that you are a serious business person that wants to grow a serious reliable and reputable company. I knew that if I wanted to be in control of my destiny, I would have to start my own company. I would be the CEO, so I could receive the benefits of all the hard work that would be required.

Even though I understood the concept of entrepreneurship, I wasn't shooting for the moon because I still had a fulltime job. I was a top performing pharmaceutical sales rep. So I really didn't have the need to build the cleaning business to be big. Although most people hate sales, being in sales changed my life for the better. It started me on the path of acquiring skills that are invaluable in business.

Learning new skill sets gave me the confidence and a sense of proudness to know that it's possible to win because I felt more equipped with the skillset necessary to go out and build a business. I had an amazing situation that took place for me while in was still in pharmaceutical sales. The drug that I was selling went generic after about 4 years of being in the industry.

When the product went generic my mental state was, "Joe you have been studying personal development and now you have the mindset to have your own business. It's time to step out on faith. "

Even though the opportunity was there I wanted to be sure that my heart was in the right place. What was more important to me was having a "WHY":

Why I wanted out of corporate America…

Why I wanted to experience financial freedom...

Why I wanted to have control of my destiny...

Why I wanted to become financially independent.

I took a snap shot of all the success that I generated while working for my outside sales jobs; the money that I made for the companies, the awards that I received for performing with excellence, the attention and accolades that I received in and for the company were in excess. I was always a top sales representative, #1 in the state and #1 in the companies. If I could do that for them, surely, I could do that for myself.

I started with a mop, a broom and a dream. The pain of not knowing if I could become successful going after my dream was more important than the pain of playing it safe by going out and look for another job. (Just over broke) J.O.B I been in the cleaning industry for over 5 years now full time and MY company has generated close to 2 million dollars in this short period of time. I'm grateful.

I take no credit. God gets all the glory. None of this would have been possible without the support of my family either. My father, before he passed two years ago, helped me out financially sometimes, when I struggled to pay my household bills, make payroll, or handle the unexpected.

I miss my dad so much. I wish he could see the level of growth God has taken me to, but I know he's in heaven smiling down, saying I'm so proud of you Joe Jr. This is not an easy business, it has its challenges, and it has its ups and downs. I've been able to employ a lot of people, help a lot of people and put them in position to take care of their families.

I'm an advocate and ambassador for the cleaning industry.

This opportunity isn't going anywhere because it's a recession proof industry. There will always be buildings that need to be cleaned week after week, month after month, and year after year. Success in business doesn't have a detector, it doesn't keep score, it doesn't approve or decline people.

What's my niche? What I'm I good at, really focusing in and becoming the best you can possibly be. I knew that I wanted to go out and build a big cleaning business. I knew I wanted to create a six-figure income for myself, so that I could sustain the lifestyle that I had grown my family accustomed to. As time goes on, you start to expand your vision and goals of what you want to achieve.

3. Desire It

Want It

How much do I really want to succeed?

Plan 1

Plan 2

Plan 3

Plan 4

How am I going to get there?

Do you think you have a weak desire or a strong desire?

If a weak desire, how do you plan to change it?

What skill sets do you have that will help you in business?

_____

_____

_____

What skill sets do you need to work on?

_____

_____

_____

What would you like to earn in your business within the next 5 years?

_____

_____

_____

Chapter Four

Decision Makers

I had a burning desire to be successful and start my own business. It was a burning desire to fulfill my dreams. I made a decision to be an entrepreneur and to succeed in it. I burned all bridges and there was no plan B. I finally decided to step out on faith not knowing that it would be the cleaning industry that would change my life forever.

I didn't know this industry would expand my mind and open up new opportunities for me. It created a new lifestyle, a fresh start and a new perspective on life.

I started my business from the ground up, no help, no resources, no mentorship, no money, no loans and no nothing. I didn't have guidance. No one was in my ear saying don't make this or that mistake Joe.

I didn't have a blueprint of what to do to accelerate my success yet there were decisions that I made that helped to advance me. Entrepreneurs are very good in decision-making. They understand that decisions affect destiny. I made a decision a few years back to embark on a journey from "ordinary to extraordinary."

Like I said in the last chapter, you begin your entrepreneurial journey by creating goals, visions and aspirations for yourself and being driven by them. I made a decision that I would focus on myself and get better.

Are you a decision maker?

It took years to learn the process of knowing how to clean buildings effectively. Being a franchise owner first was very necessary when I look back because I wasn't a business minded person at the time.

I was scared, scared of the unknown. I didn't know how I was going to get contracts from clients.

So, what did I do? I got out there and learned. You get out and talk with people. In the beginning you won't know who your ideal customer is because you will have to take any and everything you can when you are getting started. As time goes on you'll begin to get a feel for what you like to clean and who you want to do business with. If you're not in the cleaning industry you'll get a feel for who is naturally drawn to you and who you like to do business with. In the beginning, you will be doing a lot of the work. A misconception of doing a lot of the work is that its grunt work but this provides a great advantage. You want to do this for two reasons- one to get a complete understanding of the business and two, to maximize profit.

I started developing relationships in every way I could. I learned that selling myself before I sold my company was the route to success.

I also made a decision to commit to personal development and character building. Character building is expressed through the following:

- intentionally refining a pleasing personality
- insisting on a strong work ethnic
- fueling a persistent strong desire to win
- becoming a fired up and an intensely motivated self-starter
- demonstrating a giving spirit
- cultivating a willingness to learn
- becoming a believer in the power of a positive mental attitude
- the right circle of friends
- embracing a strong spiritual tradition and

- insisting on being a serious husband and family man.

I read about Julie AiIgner Clark. She was simply trying to make a video for her baby. She was unable to find any person or product that could help her. This led to the creation of Baby Einstein Company in 1997. In the first year of operation her company made $100, 000 in revenue without any advertising at all.

Passion, enthusiasm and innovation are what drove this project forward despite the limited resources. The first Baby Einstein video took off and was an instant success. It was an entirely new concept; no one had videos for babies. During the first five years, she never ran an ad. The videos were able to make babies happy. Parents told their friends. News, publicity and exposure began pouring in like the hurricane rain. She eventually sold Baby Einstein to Disney for $25 million.

Julie was successful because she saw the need for baby videos and the need produced a vision inside her; the vision shaped a product. The rest is history.

No excuses

There's one word in the dictionary I don't like at all. It's called: Excuse! I have had my own share of these. Excuses give people "good" reasons to remain in the same place all their lives. Until you excuse your excuses, greatness will be as distant from you as the sun is far from the earth.

Common excuses include too old, too young, too busy, too committed, too afraid, too poor, too rich, too tired.

Review your vision every one to three years to see if it still fits into your current dreams. Philippians 4:13 "I can do all things through Christ who strengthens me." As we all grow, develop and mature so does our life goals. Do you remember when you were young and wanted to be the president of your country, a college professor, a priest, a doctor, lawyer, crime fighter or a cop? As you grew older your desires and your goals changed too.

Do not allow excuses to cripple your destiny. The only thing holding you back from your entrepreneurial dreams are excuses.

Be a decision maker and start that business you have been talking to other people about but haven't started yet. Train yourself to be a "Yes" person.

I had many opportunities to not follow my entrepreneurial dreams. I had no money, no savings, no mentor and nobody ready to help me. I didn't even have a book such as this to inspire me to go forward and launch my cleaning business.

I made a decision that faithful day to start my cleaning business and since then I haven't looked back.

Google founders

Larry Page and Sergey Brin are decision makers. They founded Google in 1998 and hypothesized that the search engine would analyze the relationships between websites and produce better results than existing techniques, which ranked results according to the number of times the search term appeared on a page. Currently, almost 71% of all Internet searches belong to Google. I personally use Google almost every day. They made a decision to start Google even with meager means and in a garage.

"Their small company was initially called Backrub. Soon after, Backrub was renamed Google (phew). The name was a play on the mathematical expression for the number 1 followed by 100 zeros and aptly reflected Larry and Sergey's mission "to organize the world's information and make it universally accessible and useful."

Over the next few years, Google caught the attention of not only the academic community, but Silicon Valley investors as well. In August 1998, Sun co-founder Andy Bechtolsheim wrote Larry and Sergey a check for $100,000, and Google Inc. was officially born. With this investment, the newly incorporated team made the upgrade from the dorms to their first office: a garage in suburban Menlo Park, California, owned by Susan Wojcicki (employee #16 and now CEO of YouTube). Clunky desktop computers, a ping pong table, and bright blue carpet set the scene for those early days and late nights. (The tradition of keeping things colorful continues to this day.)

Even in the beginning, things were unconventional for Google.

Be Bold in Being You

Their decision to create their company has changed the world in a great way. Your decision can change the world forever.

I want to strongly encourage you to be a decision maker. Don't be one that is double minded. Don't be one that lacks the ability of decision making.

One of the greatest decisions that you can ever make for yourself is to be you. Everybody is created unique and different.

Your perspective is different from anyone else's perspective. In business there are some foundational principles that everyone should follow; your perspective is what will cause you to stand out even if your industry is "saturated".

What makes you different? I know this is a difficult question for many people to answer because it is usually followed with memories from childhood of teasing, unacceptance, intolerance and the like. But often times the thing that sets you apart when you were younger that was not accepted is the very thing that now that you are older will be accepted.

Your perspective is so important because there are people that have a similar perspective to you. In turn they will be drawn to you to be your employees, to be your customers, to be your brand ambassadors.

Those are the people you need to grow a thriving business. What they are truly drawn to is your authenticity. Your authenticity is what sets you apart and causes your business to be everything you ever desired it to be.

Truly you can win just by being you.

Footnote

Google founders

https://www.google.com/about/our-story/

4. Decision Makers

Dream It

What are the specific results I want to achieve?

___

What do I need to invest in terms of time and money to achieve those results? How much time and money?

___

What industry am I in? Sub-industry? (Product or service)

___

What do I bring to the industry or can I bring to the industry that hasn't been seen yet?

___

Chapter Five
The Habit of Consistency

I have made so much money and helped so many people along the way because of the secrets I am sharing with you in this book. One of such secrets is the power of consistency.

So many people fail when they attempt entrepreneurship because they are not consistent in their pursuit. Consistency is a virtue of the great and mighty. You've got to believe that wealth and prosperity is yours. It is your legal right.

The message and principles that are explained within this book will be a bit edgy and some principles might be new to you, but I encourage you to be patient with me and let me make my case. Read through every page carefully. I really encourage you to read this book at least three times so you can get the best out of it.

Organizations succeed because they have the right habits that make them successful and organizations fail because of their use of wrong habits. The secrets of success of mega churches and Fortune 500 companies are small habits with big effects of their founders or their employees.

For example, when Facebook was a little known social network, the founder Mark Zuckerberg decided to habitually focus on "user-experience" despite all the pressure on him to focus just on profits. That focus created habits that caused the employees to be consistent in their dealings.

That habit of focusing on "user-experience" instead of profits is considered abnormal to most but has paid off in the long run making Facebook the largest social network in the world, with almost one billion users. Myspace failed because the founders focused on money instead of its users. Focus and habits make or break individuals, nations, organizations and societies. Give any so called 'loser' the right set of weird habits and that loser will become a champion.

The habit of success

Have you cultivated the habit of success? "Normal" isn't working. The word habit is defined as an acquired behavior pattern regularly followed until it has become almost involuntary. For example, the habit of looking both ways before crossing the street or daily bathing is an American habit.

Medical dictionary defines habit as an acquired pattern of behavior that often occurs automatically. Habits are behaviors that we perform without thinking. They just happen. When we do not perform the habit we feel so uncomfortable that, for better or worse, we usually revert back to the habit.

In order to be a successful entrepreneur, you'll have to develop the habit of consistency. It is a key that will open many doors for you. Nobody wants to do business with someone who is not consistent – some days they are good and some days they are bad.

Consistency is a necessary ingredient in success. It's strange, because most people do not seem to know it's true power. It is easy to start something out of pure excitement and then over time it begins to wear out. When you have developed the habit of consistency, you will have the inner drive to continue even when you feel like quitting.

I don't even want to count the number of projects I've started and given up after the initial steam.

Even when you're passionate about something, you still have to whip out your discipline to keep going through the dips. When you get through that first valley, the results can sometimes be quite amazing.

The 5 laws of consistency

1. Discipline. Discipline helps you to remain consistent in your goals and aspirations, especially when you don't feel like continuing in your given task. When you push yourself just a little bit more each time, your discipline muscle grows.

2. Taking Action. Faith without works is dead. When you live for a strong purpose, then work is inevitable. At this point of your reading, I am sure that you've gotten so many success secrets and now you're ready to fly.

If your life has no real purpose, then you can avoid hard work, and it won't matter because you've decided that your life doesn't matter anyway. When you become driven by a purpose greater than yourself, you embrace hard work out of necessity. How many times do I need to tell you? You've got to work it. Be consistent in taking actions.

3. Abandonment. The law of abandonment is similar to the law of focus. When you abandon yourself to your consistency it will produce amazing results for you. You succeed the most where you have your most investment. Where your treasure is, there your heart will be also. It is very crucial that we invest or abandon all we've got into our life purpose to receive maximum success.

4. Reinforcement. Surround yourself with people who can encourage you and reinforce your faith. You cannot do life and business alone. Iron sharpens iron. You have to take action, but you cannot just take random action. It has to be on tasks that matter. Reinforcements are very necessary in having a consistent life and business.

5. Patience. We live in a microwave society. We want to see things happen fast. There is nothing wrong with wanting things to happen fast but you should know that sometimes great things take time to happen. It takes a longer time to cook a steak than to fry a burger. Patience is a virtue. Don't rush the process it will take to build your enterprise.

5. The Habit of Consistency

Think and Believe You Can!

What habits can you implement that will cause you to succeed?

_____

_____

Who are the people that you can surround yourself with for success?

1 _____

2 _____

3 _____

4 _____

5 _____

What businesses embody the habits or principles that mean the most to you?

_____

_____

What businesses can you emulate?

_____

_____

What "I am" affirmations can you speak over yourself to help your business?

Chapter Six

How to Start a Business

I can testify that starting your own business is the best decision you can ever make in your life. I made my decision a few years ago to start a commercial cleaning business and that decision is one that I am eternally grateful for.

Make a decision today to start your business or enterprise. Ignore your fear; abandon the safety of convenience.

Life Vision Plans are meant to be a road map; a guiding angel and not something rigid. It will help you as you begin to reinvent yourself and your business. As you reinvent yourself, your life vision may change or expand. Do not limit your destiny by sticking with the old plan.

Without goals and dreams life is bare and boring. Vision is not a material substance, so therefore it cannot be limited by physical laws. It does not respect any economic, scientific or societal laws. As you modify it and believe in it and work towards it, it will come to pass. You weren't designed to be a failure. Don't live your life as one. Even if your vision is taking time it's taking you on the path of success.

Inspire the world

The vision of flight inspired the Wright Brothers to invent the airplane.

The inventor Alexander Graham Bell changed the world permanently in 1876. He invented the telephone before he was 30 years old.

The vision of light possessed Thomas Edison to invent the light bulb.

The German reformer Martin Luther changed the world, when he nailed his 95 points against the practices of the Catholic Church, on the door of the Wittenburg Castle church in 1517.

The great inventor Sir Henry Ford in 1913 changes the world in his lifetime by mobilizing the world with the first automobile.

The adventurer Christopher Columbus changes the world as he sails across the unknown Atlantic Ocean in 1492. He is possessed by the idea that he can reach Asia by sailing west.

Our world today desperately needs new vision.

Write out your vision. It will come to pass! Invest in yourself. Spend more time and money sharpening your skills. Attend conferences, travel to different places. Get around others that are going in the same direction as you.

Don't let the negatives affect you

Negativity is an obstruction to desire. You must learn to bounce back. In the world of entrepreneurship negativity will kill your business before anyone else can or even you.

The scripture says in Romans 8:*28 "For we know that all things work together for the good of those who love God, to those who are called according to His purpose."*

If everything in life is handed to you on a fine-minted china platter, you'll never have that sense of accomplishment or the fulfillment of having achieved so much against all the odds.

I have always ensured that I have a 'success attitude' at all times. Don't let bitterness or negativity creep into your life, like a thief in the night.

Guard your heart with all diligence for out of it flows the issues of life. Don't miss the opportunity of blessing for petty stuff. Money comes and goes but true character always shines.

Get rid of low expectations. Low expectation only means a low desire. *Want your best life now! You're a child of God. Heaven has smiled on you.* You can do it.

I'm hopeful for many things of the future. Some people are afraid of the future. They go around thinking: *I wonder what my life will be in twenty years. I may never make it. I don't have good luck. My peers have done better than me and have done better in life.*

 No, get rid of those lies. You're still in the game. There's never been anyone who lined himself or herself up with God that failed. He's not going to start with you. Stay in charge of your thoughts by speaking I AM affirmations and making confessions over yourself and your business. Whenever something happens that you didn't expect yell out "plot twist" like in the movies and keep going.

Looking beyond

Janet Wilkar is a skilled and gifted entrepreneur at heart and a pharmacist by academic training. For years she struggled with working at Walgreens, made good income but never felt fulfilled. Her heart was really in starting her own business. One day she decided to quit her job to launch her ladies' cosmetics products. Two years later, she is a major force in her line of business and made a million dollar in sales.

My friend, Janet had to respond to her heart desire, even though she is a trained pharmacist, she looked beyond her 'city' her walls of profession. I wrote this book to help people respond to the higher calling of their destiny.

Robert Kiyosaki said in Rich Dad Poor Dad, a *"problem with school is that you often become what you study. So, if you study, say cooking, you become a chef. If you study law, you become an attorney, and a study of auto mechanics makes you a mechanic."*

Set Goals
...Dream It

Before you start a business, you must have a dream and vision for that business. *"Everyone is susceptible to some kind of temptation to compromise values. But there is a greater satisfaction that comes from not crossing the line. Sometimes you have to wait for [that satisfaction], but it always comes."* John Maxwell

What is your biggest dream in life? How do you make it happen? Where would you like to be in the next five years, ten years or twenty years? The third essential for success is to set goals. A big dream that seems insurmountable becomes small and attainable when it is broken down into smaller action chunks called goals. People give up on success because the vision seems so large and far away. Through the instrument of goal setting, I believe that no dream is beyond your reach.

Many of us make a shopping list but very few of us have goals list for our lives. You were not born to do everything. You can't be successful at everything. That is why you should craft goals that drive you in the direction of your personal fulfillment. The simplest way to hit a goal is to give yourself a goal to hit.

The American Society for Training and Development released this study on goal completion:
Of people who consciously decide to set a goal, 25% achieve their goal.
Of people who decide when they will do it, 40% achieve their goal.
Of people who plan how they will do it, 50% achieve their goal.
Of people who commit to someone else they will do it, 65% achieve their goal.
Of people who have a specific accountability plan and set their goals, 95% achieve their goal!

Be innovative, but you don't have to be original

Most innovators and geniuses aren't originals; they simply did what somebody did before a little better. They improved on pre-existing ideas, concepts or products. One of the wisest men that ever lived, King Solomon, declared that there's nothing new under the sun. Before Google became a search giant, Yahoo and MSN were already dominating the online search market.

Google improved on their idea and offered the world a better, easier and quicker way to search for anything on the Internet. People loved their concept and they grew rapidly, becoming a multi-billion dollar corporation.

This is a classic example of what I mean by: Be Innovative, but You don't have to be Original. I am not in any way advocating stealing or plagiarizing other people's ideas, concepts, services or products. You can always improve anything within the confines of the law and make a genius of your talents.

Make people pay for your idea

Ideas alter our world. Every day we all pay to use somebody's idea, service or product. I bet you have used one today! When you slept on your elegant bed last night, you were actually sleeping on an idea. You woke up hurriedly by the deafening chorus of your alarm clock- that too is somebody's idea. From the toothpaste you used, to the soap, fridge, coffee maker, iPhone and car, you zoomed off to work in, it was all an idea.

William Becker, the founder of Motel 6, near Kingman Arizona. On a cross-country trip in 1960, Mr. Becker needed a place to stay and he couldn't find a cheap motel room. So, he decided to start his own. The first Motel 6 debuted in Santa, California, in 1962, with 54 Spartan rooms, no closets, coin operated TV sets, and a nightly rate of $6. Today, there are more than 800 Motel 6's around the country.

I literally spent years researching and looking for a big idea that will change the world. I thought being original in whatever I was doing was the key to a superlative life. Now I think differently. There is nothing you will think of today that somebody, somewhere, and in some way hasn't done or thought about. My cleaning company is my way of changing the world. I don't do it like anyone else. I have special earmarks that represent me my company and me. That's what makes it stand out among the rest.

YouTube launched in 2005, and in few months became an instant success, sold in less than two years to Internet giant Google for $1.6 Billion. This success inspired the founder of GodTube to develop on the concept of YouTube and market to a different market - the Christian market. GodTube's growth is also phenomenal, quickly branding itself as the Christian alternative to YouTube.

You don't need to take a trip to planet Mars or vacation to Jupiter to cook up a cool concept that will baffle the world. There are plenty of creative and innovative ideas all around you!

Go for the big dream, the big life, success is yours today!

Don't start a business to fail

Do not start a business with the intent of losing money for the first three years, as seems to be the common accepted advice. Plan to make money from the start and keep it that way until your business, investment or organization grows to whatever level you desire. This advice will help you tremendously and save you money. So many people start their business wrong, practicing failure consciousness.

You may say aloud "shouldn't I be practical and prepare for the slowness experienced by most business start-ups?" Yes, I believe that you should make proper preparations for slow start-up days. Yet you shouldn't start anything expecting to fail for the first three years or until you have built your brand name, business recognition and gained customer's trust.

Before starting your business, build appropriate cash reserves (for a minimum of four months) and limit your personal liabilities. Don't go into enormous debt to start a business-do it **debt free**. I will show you how.

There's so much creativity in you. You're God's own treasure. Whatever you embark upon that line's up with your Life Purpose will definitely prosper.

Some of the most common excuses for not starting a business I have heard are:

"I'm not fit for business."

"I don't want to deal with the IRS."

"I haven't been to a business school."

"What type of business should I pursue?"

"I am too busy, I have no time."

"I'll wait for my kids to go to college before I start."

"Business is dirty."

"I have no investment."

These are all excuses that reveal a root issue, which is fear. Fear will manifest itself in different ways. Each excuse is rooted in fear and shows the type of fear you're dealing with. Either you're going to push past the fear or you're going to let fear rule your life.

This is the time for you to do something with your idea. Don't wait for all the money in the world in order for you to start something. You may be amazed how your idea can turn into a cash machine.

Bill Gates had a vision as a teenager that every business and household should have a computer. The realization of Bill Gates' vision changed the world and made him the world's richest man.

In 2002, after her husband lost his job, Green Daisy President and Founder Kim Lavine, took her kitchen table idea, the Wuvit®--a designer spa therapy pillow you heat in the microwave to $225,000 in sales in just 8 weeks. Since then she's designed a kid's Wuvit, called Sleepy-Head Fred, recognized by the Atlanta Journal Constitution as a "Top 5 Gift Pick," and has worked with Waverly®, the nation's premiere manufacturer of home décor fabrics, to design the nation's first fabric featuring a pink ribbon motif celebrating breast cancer awareness, titled "Faith, Hope & Love." In 2004, she rolled her Wuvit line out to 250 Saks Inc. stores in just 4 months, quickly followed by Macy's, Gottschalks, Von Maur, Bed Bath & Beyond, Whole Foods, and even Tabi International, a 90-store chain in Canada, taking her kitchen-table idea to millions in sales. In 2004, she was granted a license by the Collegiate Licensing Company to apply collegiate logs to her Wuvits, marking Green Daisy's entry into the $3 billion a year collegiate market. Lavine accomplished these feats of design, sales, manufacturing and distribution with little more than determination, the equity in her home and personal savings. (Wuvit.com)

How millionaires got there

Take a look at these statistics of millionaires. Envision where you would fit in.

Stock market or other investments. 65%

Paid employment or CEO type job. 58%

Real Estate. 54%

Independent Consultant/Contractor. 37%

Received inheritance of more than $50,000. 30%

Started self-funded business outside the home. 29%

Started home-based business. 17%

Franchise/Marketing/Distributor. 14%

Started business funded by others. 12%

Invented product. 3%

(Source: The Millionaire Zone by Jennifer Openshaw, Hyperion, 2007)

How to start a successful business enterprise

Starting your own business is a serious matter. Statistics show that one-third of new businesses will fail in two years. Fifty-Sixty percent will fail in four years. There are certain unchangeable in terms of starting a business. Yours doesn't have to be one of them. I am a 'how-to' and a 'bottom-line' person. That is exactly what I will do in this section. Keeping it simple and pragmatic.

1. *Your Business MUST solve a real problem and/or improve human life in some way.*

Ryan Allis started Virante, a web marketing consulting firm when he was just 16 years old. At age 22, he has helped build three companies that each generated $2 million or more in sales and a network of $10 million. When interviewed in a recent magazine, he stated that his motivation for starting a business is to help reduce human suffering and provide opportunity for all people. From Google, YouTube, my company's mission statements portray this truth.

2. *Assemble a Winning Board of Directors/Advisers.*

Surround yourself with business mentors. There are those who have gone before you and have become successful despite all the challenges they went through. You can learn a thing or two from them. Going into business all by yourself without mentorship is a risky proposition. This is why I created a business entrepreneurship mentorship program to help those who want to start a business and embark on the journey of entrepreneurship.

3. *Choose a Captivating Business Name.*

Your business name is as important as your product name. Get a name that is memorable, unique and even crazy. These names have become more memorable than the company. Think about Kleenex, Google, Wuvit, Yahoo, Myspace, iPod, Mogulus, Orkut, and Creditzilla.

You know that you've created gold when you brand or idea is very unforgettable. Your brand name got to grab people's attention

4. *Invention is not a bad idea.*

The world is ever hungry for a new invention, be it a product or service. One strong reason I believe so many start-up businesses fail is because many of them want to be "copy cats". They want to reproduce what their competitor is doing. You need to **improve** on what others are doing around you.

You don't need to offer something new, just do something better. Simply, you must brand it in your own unique way to meet the need of a particular market.

5. *Learn from the Ants.*

Think great, act small. Don't rent the premises if you can work comfortably from home, and don't hire employees until you can keep them busy.

6. *Protect your personal assets.*

If you don't protect yourself, a creditor can go after your personal assets, such as your car and your house, to pay for any debt or liability you may occur in business. Get business insurance or form an LLC.

7. Where's your Business plan?

Creating a business makes you look serious to banks and investors, as well as allows you to determine what your projected start-up costs are (how much money you'll need to save) and what your marketing strategies are and profit. If you can't make the numbers work on paper, you won't be able to make them work in real life.

8. Put all agreement in paper.

Get in the habit of getting and giving receipts for all goods, services, and deposits, regardless of how much. America is truly the land of opportunity. You can start your own business from scratch or choose from thousands of franchises and business opportunities, in practically any field you want.

Basic forms of business entities

1. Sole Proprietorship
2. General Partnerships
3. Limited Liability Partnership (LLP)
4. Limited Liability Company (LLC)
5. S. Corporation

Customer Relations:

1. Attract new customers by promising superior value.

2. Keep and grow current customers by delivering satisfaction.

Four keys to making money on the Internet

Many online or Internet based businesses fold up in ninety days. Most started with great expectations of making money online only to be heart broken and got offline since there were not making any money.

1. Find It. Your company or website should be effortlessly searchable on the net and your potential customers need to be able to find you. One common Internet myth is: A website will automatically make money for you. Having a website is like having a shop, if you don't market and promote it; people won't know your business exists, and therefore, won't patronize you.

2. Like It. Your website company has to be likable and captivating. There's as much discrimination online as there is offline. Your website has to be able to charm the attention of each visitor. Some online researchers say that your website's homepage has five seconds to grab your online-visitor's attention or you lose them.

3. Want It. It's not enough for potential clients to be able to find you and like what you have to offer. They have to also want your product. Do you have a product that people want? Could you package your product in such a way that your clients literary crave for it?

4. Buy It. I have seen individuals call me and complain that their Internet business is not generating income. Most of the time when I take a look at their websites, I discover that the sites do not follow the three master keys I just discussed. You make money on your site when your guests and customers spend money on your site. So you should make it easy for your clients to buy items on your site.

Sources of capital for your business

a. Personal savings
b. Family and friends
c. Small Business Association SBA loans
d. Conventional financing
e. Credit card
f. Home equity loans
g. Investors
h. Gift Donations

Having an excellent credit rating

a. Obtain a *free* copy of your credit from each of the three reporting companies at - www.annualcreditreport.com

b. Check for errors: This helps to ensure that it is being correctly reported.

c. Make sure that your creditors, banks, mortgage etc. report your payment to the three credit companies. If it's not reported monthly, this can affect your credit rating too.

d. Contact creditors quickly if you find errors: The Fair Reporting Act requires the credit agency to correct all errors and send a notice to anyone who has requested your report in the last six months.

e. High balances are a negative factor because lenders worry that you are living beyond your means and may not be able to repay them. Also cancelling or closing all credit card accounts you have and don't use many also affect your credit rating negatively.

f. Having a lot of available credit, even if you have no credit card debt, will lower your score, because there is a risk that you could quickly run up a lot of debt. Sadly, many people don't know this. They keep accepting every card that they receive in the mail thinking that it will help their credit power. No, it won't.

g. Negotiate your credit card debt with your credit card company. You need at the minimum one year- and- a- half to clear up records of delinquent payments, so start working today.

Common credit terms

Credit score: a score based on variables in your credit file that is indicative or your creditworthiness.

Current ratings: shows total of all account types that are currently delinquent 30, 60, or 90 days.

Inquiry date: date your credit file was requested by a third party.

Monthly payment: average monthly payment reported to the credit reporting agency- may be estimated by the agency if not reported by the creditor. (This may be indicated by an asterisk *)

Original creditor: shows the original creditor that turned the account over to the collection agency.

Prior delinquencies: date account was last reported delinquent.

***Revolving account*-**an account where a balance can be carried over from month to month.

Account status: shows the current status of your account and may indicate delinquencies that were reported in the past seven years.

Different kinds of marketing

Marketing can be done in various ways. If one process doesn't work, be flexible and use another one. Subliminal marketing is powerful and if you can't do it on a large scale like Coca-Cola does with billboards then do it on a smaller scale like company shirts, employees wearing shirts on site when performing jobs, business cards, websites, and marketing materials like flyers, banners, car magnets, logos on computers and cell phone cases.

Another way of marketing is getting in front of other people!

Advertising

Trade shows

Chamber of Commerce

Associations

Networking events

The power of no

You will be told "No" a lot but that comes with the territory. When searching for the hidden diamonds like cleaning contracts that are profitable you'll need to get through some no's to get that profitable Yes. You must understand that being told no is part of the process. You must be consistent in your prospecting.

No's provide a great opportunity if you don't get hung up on the initial rejection of a no. You can ask the person what exactly are you looking for; or what you could you have done differently for them to have said yes? If they already have someone providing the services you offer, ask what it is they are doing that causes you to keep them around. (I'll bet one of the things they will say is they are consistent.)

Allow me to be direct for a moment. If you're not making over a $100,000 a year, in your cleaning company, I want to be your mentor. If you're not making over a $100,000 in your general industry, I want to be your mentor. You need a mentor to begin to scale or upgrade your business. Until you scale your business upwards your earning potential will never go upwards.

I would like to extend an invitation to help and share some of the ideas I've learned to become financially free. Let me show you the ropes so you don't have to waste time, money, and energy. I want to position you to have complete belief the necessary concepts, strategies, and marketing techniques required to win in the cleaning industry or whatever industry you are in.

Maybe you're someone saying, "I want to leave my job and start a cleaning company." "I want to start a business on the side to pay some debt off or whatever the reason." Let me help I want to stretch your thinking I want to challenge your current belief system. I want to teach you how to go after your dreams and goals. One idea or one strategy can multiply your business and your life 100 times over.

It can take you from $50,000 to $100,000! I want to help those who believe, but just don't know how they're going to get it done. Join me we have a lot of cleaning to do, and a lot of gold to collect.

Cleaning Gold mine Nation, I am ready to serve you, but the real question is, are you ready to change your life and do what is required to make it happen?

16 tips for the consultant and service-oriented businesses

Dr. Alan Weiss is a Millionaire Consultant who started his business from home and still works at home. Here are some of his tips for starting a Consulting Business and I think it's also applicable to any business.

1. Base fees on value, not on task.
2. Never use time as the basis of your value.
3. Don't stop with what the client wants. Find out what the client *needs*.
4. Engage the client in the diagnosis. Don't be prescriptive.
5. Never voluntarily offer options to reduce fees.
6. If you're forced to reduce fee, reduce value first.
7. Ensure that the client is aware of the full range of your services.
8. If something is not on your playing field, subcontract.
9. When asked prematurely about fees, reply, "I don't know."

10. Do not accept troublesome, unpleasant, or suspicious business.
11. If you are unaware of current market fee ranges, you're undercharging.
12. Psychologically, higher fees create higher value in the buyer's mind.
13. Offer incentives for one-time, full payments.
14. Never accept payment subject to conditions to be met upon completion.
15. Practice stating and explaining your fees.
16. Always be prepared to walk away from business.

For further reading, get Dr. Alan Weiss's book "The Million Dollar Consultant."

6. How to Start a Business

Say It

What confessions do I need to make in my life?

My three biggest vision statements are?

What type of millionaire will I be?

Based on the various types of marketing techniques listed, which ones would work well with your business?

What options can you use to acquire the funds you need for your business?

Chapter Seven
The Joy of Entrepreneurship

There are many joys of entrepreneurship. Depending on who you are, and what brings you excitement, you may have different joys. I'm going to share with you my top five joys of being an entrepreneur and as you read mine, you may be able to decipher your own favorites.

#1 Personal Growth

There is nothing more exciting than becoming a better version of you. We are all created for greatness and that greatness has the opportunity to come out and express itself when we are challenged and pushed outside of our comfort zones. That personal growth becomes the catalyst of more opportunities, greater relationships and the like.

Honestly, my favorite joy of entrepreneurship is the personal growth that is required for every entrepreneur. As you begin in your entrepreneurial journey, you are just you, but as your business grows and requires more from you in order for it to grow, you begin to grow in alignment with it.

I hope you caught what I just said. As you grow your business grows. If you remain stagnant and refuse to grow as an individual, your business will stagnant and refuse to grow too. Many think that this is an implausible statement, but it's absolutely the truth. Your business, as it grows, will require to become more efficient, smarter, wiser, more aware, stronger and the like.

You literally become a better version of you. What a joy. That's what most people strive for day in and day out to become a better version of themselves. Entrepreneurs get the joy and pleasure of growing along with their business, so as they grow and begin to master more and more skills their payoff is seen directly through their entrepreneurial successes. The truth is, no one can avoid not growing with his or her business. Without growth there can be no business.

#2 Freedom

Freedom is determined by whoever has it. For many entrepreneurs, freedom is wrongly used and results in them working 24 hours a day 7 days a week neglecting their families in the name of being an entrepreneur. But that is not true freedom. That is an employee mentality now being transferred into a business.

An entrepreneur freedom comes when you are able to work and provide for your family and be there for them, which you were more than likely, unable to do when you were just an employee. Being an employer causes you to think smart, to work smarter and not harder.

#3 Fulfillment

As an entrepreneur, you should be able to monetize your purpose, your passion, whatever it is that you were born to bring into this world. So as an entrepreneur, you get the privilege every day waking up to do what you were born to do. That brings a great sense of fulfilment to your life.

As you are able to serve others with your product or your service, you are also improving the lives of others with what you have to offer. This life is made for more than just you alone. This life is composed of many people that when you have a positive effect on them, it in turn makes you better and feel a sense of joy and fulfillment that is unsurpassed.

#4 You get to change lives

How much more out of life do you need than to be a part of making another life better than it was before?

What a privilege! I don't know about you, but there is tremendous excitement that comes over me when I realize and see God's ability to use me to impact and influence the life of someone else.

To know that everything that you've seen and been through can all work together for your benefit and the benefit of others is a powerful concept. For example, you may have spent years in bookkeeping and towards the end of your career your boss started acting crazy, co-workers started changing and there was a ton of drama, you got over looked for promotions etc. But all of the experience that you acquired allowed you to start a bookkeeping business to teach others how to do it right and take advantage of legal opportunities. Or it allowed you to start your cleaning business with a great handle on keeping the books excellently. Many great companies are lost by terrible bookkeeping. All the time you were in your career you never would have thought that your pain could lead to your gain.

#5 Creating something out of nothing

The sweet part about being an entrepreneur is, you don't get bored. If you're the creative type or have a lot of skills you can use those skills, to market and advertise or add another creative facet to your business to cause it to grow.

If you're the innovative type, those innovations could lead to discoveries, innovations and creations that could change the way people live and clean. The mop isn't anything new but the most recent innovations on the mop have changed the way many people go about cleaning their homes. Think, Swifer Sweeper or Wet Jet.

Although it may take time your once far-fetched idea can become a tangible business that revolutionizes the way people live and think. As an entrepreneur, you have the power of your career in your hands. Free from the constrictions of corporate America and rigid thinkers.

All of the above listed joys are necessary to discuss because it will put your business in perspective for you. It gives you the why and encourages you to get up out of bed when you really don't feel like it.

You have to look at and stand firm on the joys of entrepreneurship when you're out and about working and growing your business. The joys must always outweigh the bad, the frustrating and the confusing.

7. The Character of Entrepreneurs

Grow It

What are the things or concepts that motivate me for entrepreneurship?
___
___
___

What areas of my life need the most work?
___
___
___

I will overcome them by:
___
___
___

What are my top 5 skills, gifts that will benefit my business?
1
2
3
4
5

Chapter Eight

6 Elements That Comprises An Entrepreneur's Blueprint

Many successful entrepreneurs and business owners do the exact same things. That's what we've learned over time. Here are the productive practices you can take away from the leaders who are succeeding in their enterprise:

1. Entrepreneurs are readers

Readers are leaders and leaders are readers. Many successful entrepreneurs I know are avid learners and readers. They have a list of their favorite books related to business that have helped them to metamorphose into the success they are today. If you are serious about entrepreneurship, you need to be curious about learning, growing and developing yourself so you can be more effective in business.

2. Create a business plan

It's been shown many times over that you are more likely to make any kind of goal happen if you actually put it down on paper. Writing down your business goals and aspirations is one of the steps to winning as an entrepreneur.

3. Get a mentor or coach

Never do it alone. I know how difficult it is to start a business without the aid of a mentor, and that is why I started a business mentorship program. Seeking the help of any successful person is extremely important, rather than just going it alone — blindly. A mentor can be a family member, someone you know in your community, an actual executive coach, etc.

4. Prepare to change mentally

If you want to grow a business, your business is only going to be as good as you are. When you invest in yourself you are also investing in business at the same time. Your business cannot be bigger you're your level of growth. Your business will become an extension of you. So however good you become is how big and awesome your business can be.

5. Be adaptable

The only thing that is constant is change. Over time the needs and demands for your business might change, so you will need to be ready to be flexible as well, so that you will remain relevant in serving your clients. Be adaptable and flexible.

6. Stay focused

Remain disciplined and diligent about what really brings in the dollars and makes your business move. Always doing new things and changing different elements around you are both important, but don't lose sight of what pays the bills — what allows your employees to get paid. Follow the steps that many successful entrepreneurs before you have taken instead of reinventing the wheel. Stay focused in your business and you will be successful.

8. 6 Elements That Comprises An Entrepreneur's Blueprint

What are the books you are currently reading?
_____
_____
_____

Why do you need to create a business plan?
_____
_____
_____

What is the importance of having a coach or mentor?
_____
_____
_____

Describe some ways you plan to stay focused in your business?
1 _____
2 _____
3 _____
4 _____
5 _____

Chapter Nine

The Art Of Selling

Selling is a big part of entrepreneurship. You do not have a business if you cannot sell. Mastering sales is the highest paid profession in the world.

Most of your CEOs were master salesmen in other corporations, organizations or their own businesses before they became CEOs. Become comfortable with telling people about your product or services. Believe in yourself. Believe in your business.

Invest in yourself and in your business. Be greedy but not in a selfish way. You'll need to understand that you have to take care of yourself before you can bless others. I guess that's why when you're flying on an airplane the flight attendant tells you to put on your mask first before you help others.

Like all other skills and abilities honed over time, selling something is truly an art form that takes practice and patience to improve.

People do business with whom they like

People do business with others they like and trust, so start with that. Before you enter into any new sales experience, make sure you bring with you an attitude of positive anticipation and enthusiasm. Anticipate learning something new — whether it's about your potential client or about the product itself. Be likable and authentic.

Be keen about learning experiences in your daily life, and keep your mind open as to what experiences might apply in future selling situations.

Use the mirror

The truth is that learning to sell can be intimidating and scary at the same time. You may lack the confidence to talk to strangers. Here is how you overcome your lack of self-confidence. Go get a mirror, look at yourself in the mirror and begin to practice your sales presentation before an imaginary business client or prospect. Practice your opening speech and how to overcome any hesitation your potential client might have. Repeat this exercise again and again until faith and hope rise up in you. You can also video yourself and review to obtain helpful hints i.e. posture, hands etc.

Have realistic expectations for yourself. Practice, drill, and rehearse the strategies until they become a natural part of your speech. Continue to study sales and test new tactics all the time. Allow yourself time to adapt material to your own style in order to create a genuine presentation and communicate naturally with the customer.

Learn to be patient

It takes time to become a master salesman or woman. Just like anything in life. It will take a few months to a few years to become an expert salesman or woman in your field. Be patient with yourself. Don't expect to be a winner 100% of the time. On the other hand, be honest with yourself and recognize times when inadequate knowledge or an inaccurate application of new selling techniques kept you from giving your best performance.

Put clients first

Be genuinely invested in the needs and joy of your client. The best salespeople are those who genuinely care about their clients. They go the extra mile to meet and exceed the desires of their clients. This business of getting what you want cannot be a totally selfish act. Your selling success increases at a significantly faster pace when your intentions to serve your clients and satisfy their needs are number one on your list. Even though you want to make more profit and more sales, you're most apt to accomplish these goals only when you put your customers first. If you make business all about making money, you will be out of business sooner than you realize.

When your clients know that you're not concerned with being the star, but that you are putting their needs before your own, they will trust you and do business with you. People are the key to your sales success.

Follow Up

Sometimes you might not close the sale at the first meeting with your prospective client, don't be discouraged. Follow up with your client. Reach out again after a period of some time and remind them of the benefits of your products and services. Give them time to think about your offer and make a decision. Never pressure your prospect into making a decision. People don't like pushy salespeople. Don't be a desperate salesperson. Don't be a stalker.

Sometimes all you have to do is to send a simple card, email or make a phone call just to say hello and let your potential customer know that you are thinking of them.

Closing the sale

Knowing how to close the sale is a big part of selling. Many inexperienced salespeople don't know how to close a sale and because of that they lose money. Many average to good salespeople prospect, make contacts, qualify, present, and handle objections so well that they manage to get by without learning to close competently. And that, of course, is what keeps them from being great. Closing contains elements of both art and science, and those elements can be learned.

Close every sale by highlighting the unique benefits that they will receive from your products and services.

Ask for referrals

You are losing money if you are not asking for referrals from your clients. After you've satisfied the needs of your client and closed the sale, you have earned the right to your next prospect. By that I mean, getting referral business from each and every client. That is the seventh and final basic. If they're happy, they'll want someone else to be happy, too. I'll teach you simple steps to getting solid, qualified referrals every time, if you're willing to learn.

9. The Art Of Selling

What are some necessary skills required to be a good salesperson?

Why is selling so important to a business?

How important is confidence in selling?

Name some of your biggest obstacles in selling?
1
2
3
4
5

Chapter Ten

Why Work With Our Cleaning Company

Healthy Environment Solutions is dedicated to being the very best customer service among residential and commercial cleaning services anywhere. While at the same time, doing our part to save the environment and protect our health. Our twofold commitment includes our sincere and equal concern for the health of you, our customer, and to the environment in which we all live.

We utilize environmentally green cleaning techniques, while providing our guarantee that we will clean your home or place of business to your complete satisfaction. We believe we are living up to our commitment to protect your health and home at the same time.

Our services

When you want a clean and comfortable space for yourself, your guests and your employees, rely on Healthy Environment Solutions, LLC. We are the best in the area. We complete commercial cleaning, junk removal and property cleanouts in Columbia, SC.

Our cleaning crew and junk removal specialists can handle everything from routine dusting to heavy furniture removal.

We've become a trusted cleanup crew in the Columbia area over the past five years cleaning apartments, homes, office buildings, restaurants, medical facilities, churches, commercial properties, senior living facilities, dormitories and more.

Each of our employees goes through a background check – so you can trust us for professional service. Don't wait another day for your cleaning and junk removal needs.

Contact Healthy Environment Solutions right now to speak with our environmental specialist.

For prompt and professional assistance, do not hesitate, call us today at (803) 457-1059 or visit us at http://cleaninghealthysolutions.com/

Our thank you

Commercial Clients

All new customers will receive a free initial deep cleaning. Refer a customer to us that uses our services and we will reward you with a cleaning certificate or 15% off commercial 1 month billing.

Bruce Lee once said, "Don't be afraid of the guy that can do 1000 different kicks but be afraid of the guy that can do one kick 1000 times." In other words, master one thing and be consistent with that one thing and become the expert

9. Work with us

Would you like to start your own cleaning business?

Why is green and healthy cleaning important?

Do you have what it takes to be an entrepreneur?

What are your 5 biggest takeaways from this book?
1
2
3
4
5

WORK WITH US

Healthy Cleaning Solutions

Call us today at (803) 457-1059 or visit
www.cleaninghealthysolutions.com

www.555success.com

www.ingramcontent.com/pod-product-compliance
Lightning Source LLC
Chambersburg PA
CBHW070201230526
45471CB00002B/759